MW01206094

EASY START

Yum, yum

Written by Keith Gaines

Illustrated by Margaret de Souza

Nelson

"Yum, yum,"
said Mum.
"Lots and lots of plums.
I like plums."

"Yum, yum,"
said Kim.
"I like plums too."

"We will get
lots and lots of plums,"
said Mum.
"We will make plum jam."

Kim got her Mum's big basket.

"Let's fill the basket with plums,"
said Mum.

Kim and her Mum
got lots and lots of plums.

"You put the plums in the water.
I will cut them up,"
said Mum.

"Can you get the plum stones out?"
said Mum.

Kim got the plum stones out.

She put the stones in the bin.

"It is like a nut,"
said Kim.

"Yes, it is like a nut,"
said Mum.

"Please can you get my big pan
out of the cupboard,"
said Mum.

Kim put the plums in the pan.

Then Mum put hot water
in the pan.

"This will make it sweet,"
said Mum.

"The jam is very hot,"
said Kim.

"It has set," said Mum.

Mum put the jam in pots.

"Yum, yum,"
said Kim.
"Lots of pots of jam."